Playing For Keeps

Books by Donald Junkins

The Sunfish and the Partridge
The Graves of Scotland Parish
Waldon, 100 Years After Thoreau
And Sandpipers She Said
The Uncle Harry Poems
The Contemporary World Poets (anthology)
The Agamenticus Poems
Crossing by Ferry: poems new and selected

PLAYING FOR KEEPS

poems by

Donald Junkins

Acknowledgments

Some of the poems in this volume have appeared in the
following periodicals:
*New Letters; The Sewanee Review; The New England
Review / Breadloaf Quarterly; The New Yorker; The Hollow
Spring Review; The New American Review; The American
Poetry Review; The Graham House Review; The Ohio Review;
The Panhandler; The New Boston Review; The Greenfield
Review; Osiris; The Little Brown House; Confrontation;
Abatis; Broadside; Salmagundi; The Midwest Quarterly; The
New York Quarterly; Willow Springs; Cincinnati Poetry
Review*

Publication of this book was made possible, in part, by a
grant from the National Endowment for the Arts, a federal
agency.

Junkins, Donald, 1931–
    Playing for keeps : poems / by Donald Junkins — 1st ed.
        p. cm.
    ISBN 0-89924-074-7 (cloth) : $16.00 — ISBN 0-89924-
073-9 (pbk.) : $8.00
    I. Title.
PS3560.U6P57 1991
811'.54—dc20   91-8498
                                                      CIP

Lynx House Press books are distributed by:

    Bookslinger, 2402 University Ave., W., St. Paul, MN
        55114
    Small Press Distribution, 1814 San Pablo Ave., Berkeley,
        CA 94702

Lynx House Press, Box 640, Amherst, Massachusetts 01004

for Theodore
who was there

Table of Contents

I.

II.

I

"We stood for a long time watching
Rain fall straight down on the
western horizon.

My right hand forgot Jerusalem
And I forgot my cunning."

James Wright

AWAKENINGS

To catch it on the upswing
brings us nearer, a kind of closing
with maple wings falling on our shoulders,
sunlight notching a familiar bracelet
on a turning wrist—to catch it

always seems childsplay
before going to the matinee, a girl's
name or the name of an herb reverberating, lovers
walking unaware of legs being two,
knowing the seriousness of glass. It always seems

an upswing, pumping a green swing riding
grapevine among alderwood: the half-open
window of a room over there, the whirr
of the hummingbird there and not there, all
the gifts of want near curtains, weight
without weight, an upswing

shaping the simplest letting go: calling
the dream's bluff. Our first gardenia
woke us from a similar sleep, loosening
hands over the dearest pond, swinging out
into the patience of lovers on mosaic cups, shaping.

LISTENING TO ERIK SATIE IN MIAMI, EASTER MONDAY

A small soggy orange at the bottom
of the swimming pool defines
the edge of an emotion that remains

into late morning, after I tossed
it for the black setter circling
the light blue wake embossed

with rippling sunlight, his eagerness
the soft, mindless, monomaniacal ritual
of exercise, after our own fifty contractual

laps, that plays against passion
and our need to simulate the intensity
of color; to know the meaning of gymnopedy

in our lives, rather than hold it apart as the Passion
itself (the quasi-modal harmony,
the unresolved chords), and it bottomed

out soundlessly as carmine
and lavender bougainvillea
give us now the color of dying:

a black bull in Seville
under the picador's lance, the gravest parody
without barlines, drawn intimately,

the withers blood bubbling in the afternoon sun,
the bougainvillea bleeding now
from the burning white stucco

westward room.

FLORENCE: A DECEMBER MORNING BEFORE SOLSTICE WITH AN INTRODUCTORY STANZA AFTER HARDY

A bright blue kingfisher in Florence
streaks along the Arno
and as I turn to watch him pass below
I see all my autumns flying hence.

Last night at the Ponte san Trinita
we heard your words in the rising head
of spring after the war from the river bed
to the marble shoulder at the *frattura*,

the fracture healed, then walked
on toward the mirror lights
holding your scarf across your face in the night's
cold air and saw San Miniato where we talked

softly down the basilica steps that first
orange night after the white monks
were chanting Latin mass alone in the sunken
cappella at the front, the bell tower buttressed

again by Michelangelo's mattresses overhead
and the bells still ringing as we touched.
We were in two places at once, such
as walkers are. "Just remember the red

of centuries," you wrote later in my book
on the inside cover. Now in the morning light
the New England autumn sky streaks below and lights
suddenly at the river's turn for a final look.

COLORS, TURNOVERS

Late Monday morning, I
cruise the yard
tied to the clothesline, my
heartstring

nagging: me
(I am two on a hot May day,
a little pronoun waiting for the turn-
over lady, my first
memory: yardtime)
in my green wool

sweater. Why won't she
lift it off? My mother
hums behind the screen
door. Over there
her blue irises

bathe in the sun. The yellow
clapboards weave
behind them in the dazzle. I
traipse between the lilies
of the valley

and the lilac tree. She's
inside whistling
before the stove, cooking
our goose. She calls:
"The turnover lady

is coming today." At high
noon, the black auto
stops. A lady carries a flat
square box in her arms. She's
walking up the driveway.

Everything disappears under the noonday sun.

SUNDAY MORNING IN FEBRUARY WITH COFFEE CUP IN HAND

watching the pair of mourning doves waddle
the deck dip-beaking to the scattered yellow
seeds, necking on the rail below
the gaunt maple branches in their addled

black-eyed watch, I think of my mother
on the move, now at my brother's
farm, chair to chair, folding her
pink Kleenex to a tiny square, over

and over working the image into a soft
wad for her pocket brood. I raise and lower
my shadow arm and the doves flap-flutter to their loft
in a nearby pine. He tries to show her

there is nothing to fear, or she
him. The inner view looks out
and the outer in. The night he
died my mother was thinking he'll wear me out.

She said that before she blanked, after
she moved eleven times. Now in warm weather
she sits in my brother's yard picking up
sticks, making little pup

tent piles. They bivouac near the high
blueberry bushes in the lower fields under
the snow. On their own, my doves fly
into the deeper woods with the snappy thunder

only game birds make winging it
home. There across the white clearing
I see my own woodpile mounds. Am I hearing
the hoo call or the silence of the final visit?

THE NEW HOUSE

We're looking for something
for the walls, holding up sketches
to the light: here's Karn's pencil drawing
when she was eight: a walrus
and a medallion dove perching
in the upper corner. *It's so deliberate,*

like Matisse (little walrus
in my office pad, I'm teaching
in the next room). *Here's the scotch-
tape from my office wall.* Our black-eyed
dove. We wander room

to room, sizing the walls,
wishing something the way we leaned
over the boat to smell water lilies,
draping them in the bow, white
spears, yellow bellies with flyspecks
in July in Maine. These walls,

translucent, snakestems pulled from lake
water, coiling as we row: we wander
room to room craving a simple scene, charcoaling
ourselves, smudging little descriptions,
framing with our fingers. Nothing

seems quite right. We're stepping
over stones, listening
with our eyes, old hands going through
the rooms.

SWAN'S ISLAND, LATE SUMMER

My daughter is making bread. She kneads
the dough. For two summers she has reached
into the blue agate lobster pan, yeasty
and flour dusty, blowing the perspiration
from her upper lip. It's her business:
enriched white, breakfast bread with raisins,
onion rye. She stirs early and late,
dumping flour bags, up to her elbows in a ten
pound sog of dough, working it over, patting
it, knifing through it, plumping

it in eight pans for the oven. Little white
fat stomachs that grow grow
all in a row. I'm in the corner
reading. Grumpy. She's Snow
White, her black hair bunned, earning
her keep. The island forest broods
in the summer heat, the lobster boats
creep around the shore at half-tide
under tiny clouds of gulls. Islands

and islands, the distraction of high
summer. I lose count of my pages,
her cupsful of flour, her summers left.
My eyes blur. I focus on everything
that doesn't count. Reading lifts me
off the page: I remember my mother
stacking the rising loaves on the radiator
under towels, my father holding a baked

loaf in his hand, smelling it warm,
kissing the topbrown crust: the fall
of 1938 before the hurricane, a different
season before the plot thickened and I left
for good. Now I'm trying to read Theodore

9

Roethke: my daughter is timing
the loaves. I daydream of fishing,
I imagine I pull up another self
from the waters I sleep on
in the dark, the pile of books I lounge

over in the mid-morning sun. I think of
telling my daughter that I love her,

ooze in the half-commotion
of half-remembered loves. I would bring
a boar's heart to the queen. She
slapdabs the tile counter with an ammonia-
soaked cloth, tidies her wrapped and warm
gambles in two cardboard boxes
and heads off.

On the table is a loaf for us.

TASTING SUMMER FRUIT, SWAN'S ISLAND

I part the high grass for strawberries
glinting in the sun, drawing
first blood: one tongue,

two tongues. Overhead, two gulls
squawk and wail: lookouts, summer
script: berry stems

soft in the fingers. Gull tongues
mimic our summer break, our ritual
code. Low thunderheads drift

west. Higher, rib clouds ease
east. The crows deliberate
on the rock beach. I recognize

the lobster boats winding
their tackle, circling under the gulls'
swarm, gunning

the throttlewash, blaring rock and roll,
the strains of early summer. You
are in a house reading,

weeding the lettuce, painting
an unfinished portrait:
peonies, wild

turkeys, the blackening peach-
seed on the corner of the deck,
the broken back-step

crawling with ants. *Distance
brooks distance.* I pick
through the grass to a strawberry

lair. The stems hold
on. Poplars rattle the breeze
just off the water, fair June.

Something arranges these roots
like hair. My mouth
waters, and my fingers stain.

THE EMPTY GALLERY

I'm in a room of late Monets,
overgrown bridges   there,

in the late afternoon cast of closing
time. I am tired. The floor

is a wall: the ceiling
is a wall. *The walls: look*

at the walls. There's nothing on the walls,
the paintings are outside: forsythia

greening, dandelions taking yellow
turns. I know the child

playing hopscotch on the sidewalk. She
tosses a piece of yellow

glass on a chalk square, jumps
over it on one foot. Down goes

the sun. *Stay inside, you must face
the wall*. I step over goldblack

ribs of frames, staring
at the white squared walls, purple

films. There a woman waves from a bridge
covered with flowers: everything is blue

white. I hold two pieces of an arched frame
around her. She whispers you miss

the point, fades into purple
green. I touch where she was. *Do not touch*

the paintings. I step into
the next room: the rug is rigid

red, fading, the walls green white. There
the bridge with flowers, orange

veils, peonies and blood
tongues. I put my face one inch

from the wall: the lines
narrow. *Stay in the white*

space. I cannot feel my feet: in the next
room I hear frames snapping. I

have been here since morning, mulling
description. My calves ache. I

lock the doors from
inside: I'm in overtime

wandering room to room, breathless
before the white walls.

LAST NIGHT I DREAMED ALL THE CELLOS MELTED

Today I stalked a deer until the snow
disappeared, helped a young woman with her play—

tonight I watch the moon meld
behind the clouds in doubleface, the way
you go and come again, your intimate hide
and seek, the way you ride
inside, perch breathing,
changeling. Don Pablo knew you inside

the strings, inside the tone bowing
the flash of *more, more,* singing
how our bodies break
each day, how our genitals give
and take away truth and mock us
in a loving, human way.

SPRING IN FREIBURG: FORTY YEARS AND MANY BOATS LATER

The old cove at Great East Lake
gives me back the dark color of water
after rain, rowing and drifting
over pickerel weeds:

the way your tone of voice seeds
softly, a slight shifting
of eyebrows to let the brain, that old sorter
of fishing days, break

through the layers of feminine
ways in other rowboats, giving me
Aunt Esther White baiting
her hook with a lively angleworm,

uncomplicated, intent with a firm
gesture dropping her line and waiting
for excitement, leaving me
free to have my own. Her genuine

content pulling in a yellow perch
with a wry smile gives me even now
the smell of the almost warm lake
in late spring, the feel of the wet

wooden seats, the way our eyes never meet
when she stares at the slight shake
at the tip of her pole, not ever wrinkling her brow:
"I've got a bite." The birch

trees over the water yards away
and the dark pines behind,
just me and Aunt Esther
fishing in the old boat "Evelyn" named

after my mother. Later I trained
myself to forget, never to let fester
lost fishing days of various kinds.
Now being free in an old cove returns the way

you do in Freiburg, the way you concentrate
on your own worm, giving yourself to me
in late spring, your free
choice, your yellow perch, your soft weight.

THE GERMAN WORD FOR CLOWN

is *Clown*. A topsy-turvy
world's a googly eye, bullseye
cheek, a heart that's upside
down. So dance my love, and dance
again under your bell-pronged
hat that crooks: halvsies

halvsies all around, the crowd
cries (it's a woman's world)
outside the *Dom*, outside
the bones of the three wise men. Even
the *Polizei* must smile

when smooched. The scene's Cologne:
carnival day. I'm the straight
man, you're the clown. Hoopla
everywhere. Gee it's fun holding
hands, snaking through the streets

before the gun goes off. We drink
beer at nine a.m., catch
chocolate and perfume at the halfway
turn, walk the littered streets
alone. The German word for tone

is *Ton*. We head for home
in Bonn, your room over the Bon-Bon
Bar beside the brothel, the church
and all the rest. You know the stuff
we do in rooms. The wine

is great. I love best
when you keep coming from the sink
saying now I must kiss you
again. Then our German

lesson. Decline to be. The German word

for comedy is *Komoedie.* Say
these words now after me: *Karneval,*
Mythe, Name, Mime,
Mann, Melodie, Wein. Say
what is this game our tongues
decline? Most endings

are the same: to complicate
is *komplizieren, verschwinden*
is to disappear. Carnival
is tricky time. The German word for dream
is *Traum.* The German word for clown
is *Clown.*

THERE IS A KIND OF GRACE

of style, the way my Patient Lucy
blooms and fades, leaving me be
as we go our ways: watering

plants in late afternoon, busy-
bodying the days snapping
stems, pushing

cylinders of plant food
into potting soil, folding off
wizened blossoms, waiting

on it, watching her heart-
shaped Impatiens' buds green,
green-pink dangling penis foils

from her ventricle hearts, now
six bloodred petals. The polyps
burst, throwing seeds, naming:

Noli me tangere. The clitorals
flair, serrated leaves abiding
in the startled air.

KITING: A REVERIE

The only play is for keeps, the way the red-tailed hawk
curls a thousand feet over the stream and hurls himself in a chalk-
line down to bunch against the magnified neck, a minuscule drifter
stark in the pebbly waters of the stream-brain; the way Ophelia

herself weeps neither for wages nor the lover's eye, leaving

the wings for good, the play forever, the irretrievable comfort of make-
    believe;
the way we drop in dreams to take
our place in the kingdom of the lost, to wonder beside the great stones
at the mica glints, the lost gazing before the shroud hovers in bones

of light over the back of our head, takes our neck in its mouth

to do with what it will; the way we drop into each other's arms
from the day's events, the hours polishing the table at the empty farm
    turning our
throats to the mouth's kisses, the goddess come again
for the love of gods, for mercy's sake, the human dream.

This must go on we say, this keep-in-touch, this tangled play

of lobes and nipple-burls, this fingering light
play of flesh opening and closing down from a great height,
handing ourselves over—oh, yes, to the hawk's breath
on our fragile neck, and our tongue's stealth.

II

"Our souls are in our children. I have always known it."

Andromache

Euripides

HAULING TRAPS WITH THEODORE: A MIDNIGHT NARRATIVE AT LOW TIDE

The flashlight dangling from my neck
keeps dying. I am eyeing
the low places, trying
to keep upright in the wet rock-

weed. We're at the edge
of an eleven foot tide
just turning. On his side
(one foot slipping a low ledge)

my son Theodore taps the sea-
water from his light
until it flares. The night
fog silkens in the beam. He

answers "I'm OK" when I call his nick-
name through the dark
and scan my light to mark
his fall. "Thee," I call, and pick

my steps across the shell-
crushed white of the low tide
cove. "Yes," he says beside
me. My youngest son. His name tells

me what I have to know. When
I am old it will be
between us, this benediction of the foggy
cove, these periwinkle agate bells ten

times ten under our feet
as the rush of the wavelets breaks
at our knees. We make
our way to the weighted lines seated

in the crevices of the low-drain
ledges. "Here's one," Thee
says as I shuffle waist-deep toward the lee
of the inland cove. This is the Maine

coast, the summer of my
last son at home. My light blinks on,
off, on. I can see kelp flowing silky brown
through my ankles. I

reach now for the floating black
line. Thee whispers from his trap, "Two,"
as I haul. "You
better bait," I call, our voices flowing back

to back, face to face across the heavy
swells. Intimacy,
the declension of father and son, Thee
and I, second persons familiar. We

work in quiet. I lift
a keeper and a short to the clam roller, re-
bait and heave the wire trap to the sea.
A blush of bubbles, it sifts

down, gone. We haul
the other three and mount
the broadbacked ledges. We count
the summer's haul: secrets. "I'll haul

anytime, day or night," Thee
says. Inside, we take off our wet
boots and shorts, stack split
spruce in the fireplace. We

talk: now and then: fog, bait,
my father's lobster-onyx ring. In
the refrigerator produce tray, the blackening
lobsters wait.

YOU, PAINTING IN ANOTHER ROOM, ANOTHER TOWN

day after day. On the wall our mayflowers
twine the beeswax leaves, wax
earth: brown, creamwhite, tint of pink: the color
of the ground in spring crossing
over,
　　　　the watercolor deer
with the spider antlers and the black bulls-
eye leaping every day beside the reaching
nude. You skipped

whole conversations, spring, summer, painting,
painting: then you sat up in bed
in September after we did it, shaking your head,
smiling, *You can't beat that.* We ran two miles
to the brook and walked home past the juniper slope,
the peeper swamp.
　　　　　　This morning
I got the good seeds for the bird
feeder. Both cardinals came. Then I ran
to get it over with. I miss you
getting your grip, your *purchase*
on the long hills.
　　　　　　You spoke
of big birds with such reverence, how
the great gray owl whispered over your head
within inches, veering
into the pines. You painted giant
lemons. In June after running,

working the huge still life with irises
and grapes in a dish of tangerines, you
said *Mourning doves are the dumbest
birds I know. This morning I saw one fly
from the road to a branch and teeter.*

RUNNING WITH MY SON IN GERMANY,
REMEMBERING MY FATHER

The rain in a motion of images sweeps
and blows us running through the Black
Forest, the cool reminders on our thighs,
the invisible blood yearning toward brightness:
the giant cardboard sunflower in my father's
room between the bed and the dresser, catching
the windowlight flowing in over Mrs. Hammerstrom's
pear tree, a Kansas sunflower stalking me
still, my father's plaything in the bedroom,
his Republican Party, Alfred Landon sprouting

petals all dressed up in a burst of flower
yellow. The rain spatters my brow in cool sheets: now
a light mist on the forehead. A hawk
who saw us coming is gliding
to another idea, another branch. I
am fifty, running in this other land, bringing myself
around. I see the sunflower from that old presidential

campaign in the thirties brightening the room
where I was conceived and born and watched
the doctor who delivered me sew up my father's
thigh from the cow horn, threading,
needling: no anesthesia for my father. I
wait out my German measles, try on my seven
dwarf masks, smell his old cologne on my fingers,
touch the sun flowering in giant card-
board. One morning I hand him the *Boston Sunday
Post* blaring the Coconut Grove fire, 500 dead

inside a revolving door, even Bobby Benson
the cowboy on my red Wheaties dish. The room,
yellow in the rain, yellower than these fresh
stacked maple logs, cords of yellow bulls-

eyes looking the other way, the room I'm
running from and running to with the drawn
curtains, a certain yellow light there and not
there, running with no sound in the rain. Up

ahead I will turn around and start home, my
seven miles, just so far
and no further, my son at my
side. Last week he told me that once running

alone he thought about dying
and stopped. We are taking
turns. We are passing beehives,
yellow boxes in a field of saplings. The rain
softens our path running, running
toward the sun.

A PASTICHE: THE TRUTH THAT FALLS FROM THE SKY IN DEERFIELD, LATE FALL

Down back of the house in the November woods
a man and a boy eye the high limbs for squirrels
running against the last brightening of the sky.
The shapes of things draw darkness
from the woods and seem to stir
as night comes on.
                When the man holds out his hand
they hold their steps—and slowly turn
their heads to stare back the roosting partridge
into the nub and hump of a beech limb, dark
against the sky.

Dark the sky, darker the image on the mind

The boy relaxes his grip on the .22 rifle,
turns his eyes to the treetops, pushes
the trigger safety off and on for something to do
with his fingers. Down a slope and the oaks
are pines (he would fire the gun
at a stump for the sake of it, but the man would call
it waste) and the boy sees the squirrel's nest
snug against the crotch of limb and trunk: "Can
I shoot into it? Maybe one's lying down—"
Neither questions what they think they see.

Stumps, targets, trees: the hunter sees

The boy's shot slices the silence of fall.
Standing beneath the tree, he
shoots straight up and the man wonders
if a bullet will fall back down on them (last
week the boy asked where do high bullets fall? The man
said they fall easy, way off). The gun
cracks again: something moves (a squirrel's
tail flickering in the nest?) Bang!—the gun speaks
four times.

30

Gunning for truth as near as death

Suddenly the top of the tree is falling
toward the boy—a great weight crashes down
through the dead spikes of branches: a gunny sack full

of dark sky, a great oval stone, the bear
from the stars above the trees. The boy ducks his head,
twists his shoulder out of the way,
the heavy sack clumps the ground beside him.
Two squirrel hunters stare—

The bear in the sky, the sky is falling

"What is it?" the boy asks, and sees it falling again
from the top of the tree.

Falling all fall down—can't catch me can't

They both know—
a raccoon, by the stripes, and the father sees
the sadness in the son's face. "What
should we do with it?" the boy asks, plain
that he thinks of the animal alive.
"People eat raccoon"—but the boy shakes
his head in silence and the man says they better
leave it there for the crows, something
that can get the good of it.

The good crows, craw crawing

The boy keeps his thoughts
as they walk up the slope. Each had saved this last
hour of light for the other, now each has it
for himself. Fooled by the darkness in the light,
they walk the darkness home, a steady pace
to leave the unexpected in the woods. Twice
the man says softly it wasn't the boy's fault, twice
the boy answers he didn't know what was coming
down at him.

THERE'S A MULBERRY BUSH

somewhere, all the unborn children
skip around it, holding stubby
hands in the early morning
sun, dancing blubbery thighs
under long Monday dresses, bow-legged

under high Tuesday stockings, arch-pink
insteps under buckle-Wednesday boots, and so
on. The ground is air,
happy nofaces waiting
to be born, hopping, toady

gnomes dancing their turns
for faces, every girl Patience,
every boy Mark: there they go
round the mulberry bush stomping
cheer, gliding in airy

hope. Each girl hums *I can be
a she*, and wonders
about the other ones, dancing
feet and holding hands so early
in the morning. Each boy

hums *I can be a he*, arabesques
and wonders too. As quick as one
is gone, another jumps from the bush
hands out and dancing feet, a noface
knowing, a noname humming:

Rubensesque, round and round
a little berry mulling.

A NOTE TO THEODORE LEAVING FOR AMERICA NEXT WEEK

You are at the Freiburg lake on Saturday
afternoon. I'm in my office down
town above the streetcars, the spring
chestnut trees. Once you said if we do not live
together it would not be a tragedy, and I
said no but I meant yes. I see you
coming across Sam Melnick's field two falls
ago, your shotgun

over your head in one hand, the cock
pheasant dangling high
from your other: the corn ploughed
under, the new blue silo
dazzling in the clean air, the smell
of sour mash everywhere: he went up
three times and you nailed him
over the gully after you got the shell
in the chamber, after you got the safety
off. We saved the tail

feathers, the photo
in the driveway, even your license
stub. Yesterday in the Moss
Forest, running, I heard another cock
squawking. We could have flushed
him near the beehives but he was not our
bird. We bang around
in other fields: by the tobacco

barns in Sunderland up Bull
Hill Road, behind the fish
hatchery, Laurenitis's potatoes, the river
road in Deerfield: getting the lead
out. You are going home my Patrick boy, my black and tan,

my Russian, my German, my Scot
sidekick, my island

prince. Goodeye. I'm
your bird. When your second cousin
Ralph Haywood left for the war, my
father said stay with'em boy.
I'll stay right on top of them.
He was killed in a jeep in Germany. Now
we are here in another spring, no
guns. Advice is for

the birds. So, my advance man, I'll
follow you home after the landscapes,
after the words.

I KNOW A CHILD CALLED FORTH

from the dancing land, I, a begetter
of bees, who could not keep
the bear from scrambling the bulging
hive in winter, in the near woods
beyond the briary hedge, I who BB-ed
the chipmunk in the spine at the base
of her stonewall house, I

who said yes to the frog princess
who wanted to dance herself,
who padded the lily pads, bug-eyed
for air, who curled in a ball,
a begetter of names, and curled
the names from our bee-tongues

forking, forking in the mouth-air
of the grandswamp lair, I who walked
the hospital stair to the white room—
where oh where—and I, too, the assenter
of names, sent the child home
with no supper, I, a begetter

of air.

UNFINISHED BUSINESS AFTER DARK

We cast for bass along the pitchblack
shore, rowing and drifting, plop-

ping our jitterbug and fake field
mouse, our ritual of tiny

plays: cast, reel. The overhanging
pines cast deeper shadows

than the dark. Gurgle, gur-
gle goes the bug. The mouse moves

barely to the tip
of the tipping pole: gliding

in the dark, listening for the cock-
sure smash of the black

bass: the plug snags
a drooping pine. *Drift. Drift*

in. We finger the branch-gagged
hooks, row the dark

water, cast the night mist. *Feel
how warm the water is.* Dipping

our fingers, we head for the opening
of the cove: believe bass, be-

lieve. This is the way the darkness
goes: black night, big-

mouth black bass, we
will be back tomorrow night.

EPITHALAMIUM IN THE BRICK CHURCH, DEERFIELD

Spring keeps coming through the elms: old
dowsers bending in the May
wind fingering over the gray
namestones, the honeysuckle bushes, marigolds

after rain, after the names
pass on. Pass it on, the names say
in the silent hiss of the eraser wind, the play
of stop where you are when you can't, the game

of hold hands, walk circles, all fall down
under the drowsing elms. The names say:
say yes to whatever's up in the May
wind, in the fields at the edge of town

where we headed north and the ducks now
rest in the rushes, say yes the only way
a body can: touch kindly, pray
for simplicity, take notice how

Jack stands alone in his pulpit, valley lilies bell
in beds, rue takes care, May-
flowers root for keeps. Spring keeps saying
come, come on, the elms are tolling, telling,

turning water into wine: Cana
in Deerfield where the names this spring day
give us our selves, where our words, our clay,
become flesh under this gold weather vane.

III

"I am no longer hunting for shells of bygone streams. I am searching for something far more mysterious. . . . It is found at last at the most forlorn hour of the morning, when you have long since forgotten that eleven or twelve is about to strike, . . . And suddenly, as one thrusts aside bushes and briar, with a movement of hesitating hands unevenly raised level to the face, it appears in sight as a long shadowy avenue, the outlet of which is a small round patch of light."

Alain-Fournier

Le Grand Meaulnes

PLAYING GLASSIES WITH DICKIE MALLAR

Alone in the garage, I work my hand
through the floppy topcloth of my marble
bag and squeeze whole handsful of little glass
balls, dribbling them on the pile
in the metallic dark. I know the crystal balls
by heart, swirls of cream and raspberries,
here a wine red, here a buttercup yellow streaked
with devil's grass. May: the marble season. I

carry the sugar bag around
the neighborhood after school, plopping
it in backyards, calling for takers. We
gouge holes with our heels in lawns,
driveways, sidewalks, earth gutters. We
scoop fistsful of dirt with our hands,
pat the edges of our holes with our finger-
tips. Closest to the hole shoots first. Tucking
my thumb against my curved forefinger
I nub the sweet rolling glassies
into the hole, every one. I never lose. I
am Midas Junkins the glassy king. One

day, Dickie Mallar walks up from Blue
Ridge Road and stands in the street outside
my house; "You got any
glassies?"
        "Sure."
"You want to play?"
                He digs ten giant purees
out of his pocket: he'll roll against everything

in my bag. One by one he fingers them
in the late afternoon sun: blue bachelor-
buttons, orange poppies, copper green lily
pads—the colors are so rich my belly

churns with a lover's passion. Mallar
keeps throwing them: candlewax

black, burnt-pumpkin belly
black, the black eyes of the new girl
on her back in the field staring
sideways—Mallar rolls them all

and loses every one.
                        When it is over, his risky
debonair ways puzzle me. "What's
a glassy?" he says and walks
home in the dusk. I feel cheated. I
have everything in the bag.

                        I stash
my glassies in the garage. Behind
closed doors I finger them
in the dark.

PLAYING WITH FIRE

On a windy Saturday morning in the spring of 1940 Charlie Blood
crawls with me through a low lattice door and we hunch
in our mackinaws under Charlie's front piazza, staring
at the sun-slits on the dirt floor. "Let's get a lunch,"
Charlie says, "and eat it here." I try for Wonder
Bread across the street ("not until noon") and crawl
back empty-handed. "She was in the kitchen," Charlie
says, "This is all I could get," lifting an ivory
rectangular salt shaker from his coat. He shakes a pile
in each of our hands and we take turns lapping until we
have to give it up. Charlie fishes two wooden matches
from his pocket: "We can get warm with a little fire." A few
thin twigs and a piece of broken lattice are burning good
when my mother sees the smoke and gets my brother's belt.

When the welts on my legs calm down, I go looking
for Charlie. I find him in Wormstead's field with Arthur's goat.
"Let's go out in the woods," I say, and we jump the low-hum
electric fence on the other side of Fairmount and walk
to the top of Pirate's Glen where Kidd, people say, buried
gold when The Valley was a river before the earthquake. At
the slit-mouth of the cave I balk but Charlie starts in
on his back feet first, his turned head, through the ten inch
opening, disappearing into the dark. When I get inside Charlie
is burning book matches one by one until they are gone: we sit
in the dark, leaning against the damp rock wall. No one knows
where we are. "We need flashlights," Charlie says, and we hike
home. I rummage the cellar

and the dining room commode: no luck. Charlie
says he couldn't get past the kitchen but snuck half
a box of blue birthday candles: inside the cave we sit
in the flickering light. Charlie drips blue wax and sets
the burning candles on a rock. We watch them burn down one
by one. The thin candles glare in the hollow silence. Dim

light. Dimmer. Blackness. We smell burnt wick in the dark,
ten feet underground. We can't do a thing about it. We crawl
into the spring light and run between the piss oaks
burgeoning with yellow green leaves. We slide down Slide Rock
on our backs. We look for blacksnakes under boulders. We skip
stones across the cow pond. *If the salt has lost its savor
wherewith shall it be salted?* We chase Tom Mahan's ganders
until they turn hissing:

go back go back. We hunt
early columbine. Empty-handed we scale a leathery cowflap
onto the South's front lawn. This Saturday in the spring
of 1940, Charlie and I are nimble, we are quick. We strike
our flint and kick the bushel. We are spring, jumping over
everything. We are candlewick flaring in the wind.

A CHEER FOR JANICE WEIR THIRTY FIVE YEARS LATER

You are just a pint
of peanuts, I am ga-ga
up the street, all the president's
names under our feet: down
Cleveland, down Harrison, down Garfield,
and Washy and Jeffy. After dark
that first spring, we learn stopping
and kissing all the walk

home: your back
porch with the yellow wooden
rail. Sadie says nix
on going steady. One night I trail
you in my father's '38 Buick
and wait for Charlie Prentiss
to bring you home. You run
up the front steps and in. The light
goes out, I drive home. Then you

faint at school, I
carry you to the nurse's
office, fall asleep afternoons
across the end of your bed. You
are doing algebra. I never know
what you are sick with. Once,
we play our clarinets in Dorr Memorial
Church, and I squeak. You
pretend you never heard. You
slip the five into my wallet

on the Everett to Boston MTA, I
do not figure it for a month. I
am slow on the take, slower
on the give. When you fall
for Richard Hennigar, I will not come

home from college. Even minister
Udy from Australia cannot get me
to eat. You cry in church, I
screwball off in a soggy

dream. Dear Jan with the over-the-shoulder
look, we touched
only with our mouths. Pert,
quickeyed, you ran
like a fawn, arm-wrestled like a Japanese
flyweight. Accept if you will
this cheer, and another, and three,
in my fiftieth year up the long
long street.

RUNNING THE BUCKEY ON WORMSTEAD'S POND

In the hollow below Wilfred South's house
we show up for hockey at "Wormy,"
the cow pond. The Valley ice is black
thin, no one dares skate,

then Buddy Frederickson starts across
edging and slipping, laughing that no
one else dares do it. Ralphie Romano
takes a headstart from the low bank grass

on the cow road and runs past Buddy, white
cracks streaking tiny lightning in the dark
glass. I watch them form the line, light-
headed, holding my dog Pickles, barking,

barking. I have ideas: no black ice.
Wormy is my summer pond: I stocked
the hornpouts at the cold dark
bottom, spring handouts Paul Baldwin netted in Sluice

Pond for pickerel bait, slipped to me
when they outgrew his glass tank. (I
can see the five foot blacksnake writhing
on the surface, over and over: Charlie

Blood keeps flipping it back with a clothespole
until it sinks.) "Let's go Ranny!" "Come on
Ray!" Arm in arm they stomp the coal
black ice over Wormy, whoop under the morning sun

and start back: four buckeys before Charlie
Maes's foot goes through and they have
enough and stomp up Fairmount so Charlie
can change his shoes. The ice is still wavy. I

stare at the hole where Charlie's foot went through:
a pool is spreading on top of the ice
over the once flashing cracks that held like glue.
Am I safe on shore? —looking at the white ice

turning dark again—can I get to the bottom
of it? I sit beside the golden tall November grass
watching after their young autumn ways
with my old summer eyes.

SLIDING ON BARN HILL IN THE DARK OF THE STORM

We bite the ice balls off our mittens with our teeth,
run head starts and belly-bump our Flexible Flyers
down past suppertime. The snow turns to sleet, Keith
Berry cries "It's getting slipperier and slipperier!"
and races Rusty Hultzman to the McGann's front
steps. One more run, just one. Rusty is game:
sweaty, played out, on a dare he touches the blunt
of his tongue to his sled runner, a piece of skin comes
off but he's happy. "This is the nuts," he
says over and over, and soon: "I gotta go home." One
by one the ice-crusted players drift off in the dead
of the storm. I'm alone with Janice McGann: "Fun, fun"
she says and breasts her sled before me down the hill,
and up and down again before I tackle her—
"Let me go," and I do, and run with my sled until

my ice-clogged overshoes drag me down. A blur
of icy wool shoves in my face, then against my naked throat
a winter wooly crab ice-pinching—I grasp
my frozen claws around her; "Let me go," our lobster coats
buckling: shedders in December, out of season in the rasp
of winter. I will not let her go as the sleet turns to hail
on little Barn Hill ten miles north of Boston in 1945. Janice,
I kiss you still, the ice pelts our foreheads blue snails,
waves of small round snails bouncing and rolling, alive
on the glassy crust, pelting our short quick kiss, our light
kiss, our melting icy kiss, and then I let you go—
and then I let you go. Down we crunch toward the bright
lights in the houses below and say "So long," "So
long," in the dark. I drag my sled past the high street
lamp at Sherman and Cleveland as the hail burns into sleet.

CHILDHOOD, THE GLASS CRYSTAL

My yellow school, my yellow
childhood, my birches in the playground
my seagreen swings, my stone
running place:

> Miss Bridgham
claps her hands on the school balcony
porch: recess over. The girls play
the field along Cleveland Avenue,
the boys play Fairmount. No one
may enter the birch grove. Near

the swings, Dickie Mallar shows
me his glass crystal, fast, before we go
in, holds it above my wrist, holds
my wrist tight with his hand: *Keep looking,*
you'll be surprised,
> the sun burns my skin, I
pull my hand, shake it, tears
in my eyes, *You goddam*
Mallar (laughing,
putting the crystal back in his pocket)
Miss Bridgham clapping *Come*
girls, come boys. Years

later, walking home from the senior
play with senior Evelyn Kenney, my first
ninth grade date, we meet Mallar
at Elm and Blueridge. At the end
of Sterling he is in the middle, cocksure,

putting an arm around, saying something
in her ear: Evelyn
pulls away *not tonight.* At the end
of Fairmount *goodnight boys* she walks

the rest of the way alone. The next day
at band practice, Esther Gibbs fumbles through
the baritone solo until Mr. St. Germaine tells
Mallar to play it. Dickie can really play
the baritone. He never misses a note.

HORSESHOES IN SAUGUS

The summer evenings hang over our heads like warm
damp cloths: the gardens are in,
the news is on, the war, that single black fin,
lounges across the seagreen summer evening light.

Supper is over. My father sits beside himself
on the porch steps, thinking of trenches, the Marne,
my brother seventeen. I walk up Cleveland to the Maes's barn,
lift the horseshoes from the twelve penny nail.

The moist yellow evening light drips through the apple
leaves in the lot across from old Leander's house
where they built the horseshoe court. Ray douses
the dirt clay black and Ralphie rakes. We pack

it in like a colony of ants in lock step. The whole
neighborhood is there for something to do, two
against two before the older boys go off to
war: the silver shoes against the gold.

Dickie Maes plants one foot against the front board
of the stakebox and underhands the horseshoe
as if he is pitching fast softball. The shoe
turns once, a perfect upside down loop, clangs

against the stake in the open U and bounces back
three inches dead in front of the iron pipe. Dickie
says *shit* and aims the second shoe. He
holds it with both hands, arms outstretched, peering one

eye through the open prongs as if it is a slingshot.
Everything is at stake. It all adds up to twenty-one.
The second shoe drops a thousand times and wins
some points and loses some. Is it the silver or the gold?

The color has worn off even now. We have light
on our hands two hours before dark. We take our time
and toss it back and forth. In this old limelight,
style wags the tail even among brothers:

Ray Maes stands outside the stakebox and lets the shoe go
on the upward swing of his forearm, turning
his wrist ever so slightly, turning,
letting go the shoe for a two-and-a-half-turn opening

as it approaches the stake, turning a little, hooking
on, iron grabbing iron. Such form. Such grace.
One night Ray throws five ringers in a row: Ray Maes
the champion. Al Ripon walks up from his house

at the cheering. And Ralphie Romano, my partner: squat
Ralphie, sweet-tough Ralphie who curses the green
sun when he misses and lifts his finger in obscene
display and stamps his foot. Rumpelstilskin Romano.

When the green sun sets and the apple leaves turn
black and blue by Ripon's garage and we can't tell
the stake from the backboard, we mill around to tell
stories under the black maples and then walk home

under the moist green stars. Charlie Maes dies in Africa
in 1943. After the war Dickie marries Marie: they
live in the remodeled barn. Nobody comes to play
horseshoes in the evening. After the ninth baby, Dickie runs

away. We too have all run away in the dark. Someone
built a house on the horseshoe court thirty years
later. Cleveland Avenue is quiet now. Two more wars
have crowded out the fields. Whatever was at stake

takes on that summer's evenings and those cheers.

PICKEREL FISHING

The white pines drip green over the dark road
to the spring and I saunter in my tilting
swinging gait, lop-headed as the milk can
tinned the color of bronze weighs my right
arm down, swinging the can, Indian quiet
on the pine needles eyeing the clumped green
edges of the powdery summer-burnt dirt road
watching for frogs, daydreaming of the sleek
pickerel in the nearby cove, going for spring
water. I am five. I am a pickerel myself

dreaming of a lady pickerel lounging
in shallow warm water, her frog hungry
tongue on hold, amputated arms brushing imperceptibly
like a runner folded at the starting
gun, drowsy and beagle-eyed in her green
and yellow casing, casement black,
her long muscle alert to move in a lightning
stab and the long chew, the frog's leg
dangling from her lockjaw, disappearing

into the maw like my father sucking a drop
of tobacco juice at the corner of his mouth
into the plug inside his mouth, chewing
in the sun at the other end of the boat
watching the water, and me watching
the water, holding my long bamboo pole
toward the quiet water where the swirl
occurred on the path to the spring

dizzy with August, mosquitoes rising
from my feet on the damp path, dragging
my can in the shallow spring, riling
the bottom, eyeing the wood frog goggling
two feet from my hand, swiping my left

hand in front of his nose the way you lead
a duck pickereling up from a grass quilted

slough, his feet dangling from the mouth
of my hand and I put him in the can
and clomp the tin cover on. Back
at the camp my Uncle Harry asks me
if the tumbler is still on the stick
and I think it is a joke, what

is a tumbler and he says "tumbler"
again and then he takes off the lid
and sees the floating frog and swears
and my father laughs. All I can think
of is a clown tumbling at the spring

and me grabbing the spotted brown blur
in mid-air. I am fifteen before I know
a tumbler is a drinking glass. For years
it is there upside down and I see it, then

it is gone. My Uncle Harry and my father
are gone too. Last summer I cleared
the leaves and sticks that clotted

the spring with no goggling frog
but someone had placed another tumbler

on an old broken stick.

IV

"He came here a-fishing, and used an old log canoe which he found on the shore. . . . He did not know whose it was; it belonged to the pond."

Henry Thoreau

ROBERT LOWELL: THE CHURCH OF THE ADVENT, BOSTON

The Chinese organist booms out six preludes
in the high episcopal church: Lowell,
our old teacher, is dead. Outside
a blue rainbow crowns imagined Boston, our old
city.

Our old class is here except for Anne
who closed the garage door on her wrist.
From the back pew I can see the backs
of our heads, bent to the mimeographed
poem in our hands, puzzling over the middle
that goes haywire—why doesn't the ending
end?

Lowell, our old
rainbow man up front again, inside
the pickerel eyes, untangling the whole idea.
He's not old, he's brand clean olive
drab in his new khaki gabardine teacher's
suit. His head holds the creases
of his sleep-sogged bed. None of us
can speak. Lowell's mouth is open—
moving, the old-new words cut through
our dumb show, spilling the words of his deadly
wits, his soft whine
marking over the lines of our poem: summer
falling for Philip Larkin on the page,
an hour before tea, what isn't said. Lowell
smiles his Mona Lisa smile: "a cozy time. . . .
not much to celebrate." Larkin is "infinitely
guarded."

We're guarded too. Lowell
passes out poems: Allen Tate, Ivor

Winters, Robert Graves ("It's a small
tornado.") Snodgrass writes to Janice
that the old scars darken in the autumn
weather. Lowell circles the phrasing, moving
in and out of the poem, phrasing himself,
trying to nail down what makes it
happen. Reading out loud, he names the locust
husks, the grass where we all had gone. He
muses, fumbling away from overkill: "softly
symbolic."

Now the neoclassical notes of the German
composers slambang from the high stone
walls. All our heads are stone still,
listening, not hearing. Only the editor's
wife turns to watch for the wives,
the undertakers, the mahogany body passing
underneath the vestments, too fagged out
to ride anymore sitting up in the cab, floating
on rollers soundlessly down the aisle canal,
the Harvard pallbearers wading behind.
The mahogany rests in the still waters
of the nave, the longboat at mooring.

—Eating his bag lunch, staring out the window
at 232 Bay State Road toward the shells
on the Charles, he doesn't see me in the office
doorway, helpless before class, gone
on my goggle-eyed mentor, blurting:

> "I just read *The Mills of the Kavanaughs*,
> I think you're better than Eliot."

He focuses me, almost smiles. I've said something
unimaginable. He manages the space
between us awkwardly, squeezes my shoulder,
shakes my shoulder slightly, walks across
the room as if in a dory, sits awkwardly—

In the church the beefy censor strides down
the center aisle swinging the smoking urn
to the right, out to the left—incense
curls into the mass for the repose of the soul
of Robert Traill Spence Lowell.
                              Everything
is stuck in my throat. Someone is reading
in the pulpit from *Isaiah*: the Lord will make
feasts, fat things, wine
on the lees well refined. There is high style
here, grace.

—At McLeans they open three locked
doors: I step into his room overlooking the fair-
way, step toward him in my charcoal
gray suit. He starts toward me in his blue
turtleneck sweater, overweight, bulge-eyed,
frazzled; lifts his fresh pencil portrait

by Ann Adden from the bed, do I like it?
He corners me, what do I think
about God? I stall, he says, "You mean
everything just the way it is?" He tugs
"Waking from the Blue" from the typewriter,
hands it over. I read out loud, smiling: "There
are no urinous screwballs in the Catholic
Church." He smiles, "There aren't"—

The psalmist is saying we will not fear
though the earth be removed. I look
at my hands. Later he changed *urinous*
to *Mayflower*. I'm all ears. I'm trying
to say goodbye.

—When I was a child, Simon said do this, do
that. I took ten steps ten miles north
of Boston.

Around the corner from Revere
Street, I'm listening as hard as I can:
the reader MacKay is quoting *Revelation*: John
hears a great voice; there will be no more
death, former things are passed away,
a voice says write. I imagine Lowell stepping
into the land of the dead like a stunned
bird. He brings William Merwin to class
on Merwin's thirtieth birthday and asks him
to read a new poem. Merwin reads two he wrote
the day before. Lowell says, "My newest
poem is three years old."

Then he makes a comeback. Pound's
postcard tickles him. He reads us
the opening before class:

> "Mr. Robert Lowell of Boston
> no Baby Austin. . ."

He grins for the old class in the history
seminar room of Boston University on Common-
wealth Avenue. He rhymes Boston and Austin
in his soft vibrato whine, his old whispery
insider whine, his child seed whine, stomping
with grandfather, sipping sasparilla. Now
he has something. I tell him after class
one day: *"Lord Weary's Castle* is terrific."
He says, "I have some new ones

that are better." He sends a batch to Pound.
In class he praises Pound's wit, scoffs
at himself, delights in the limelight
of it all. He is famous again at forty.
We spend an hour on a six line poem
by Robert Graves before the morning mirror
shaving.

Now it's late morning in mid-September: Brimmer
Street. The sanctuary is dead still
before the homily begins. Our only adjective
for quietude is dead. No voice, no
sound. No one coughs. Patience,
the devil's undoing. Passion
honoring time. I remember the lines
in his face. I am 45 years old. No one
is moving a muscle:

—Riding the elevator before class, I
tell him we are going to name our new
baby Bray Robert, after him. Lowell
chuckles from the back of his jaws,
as if chewing: "You mean 'bray,'
like a donkey?"

Behind his back we call him Lowell
as if it is his first name. He passes
out sheafs of xeroxed student poems, jumps
to Swift in the *Viking Portable Anthology,*
shuffles in Frost's "Pauper Witch of Grafton"
to see if we recognize it. Class is pure
method: stick with the poem long enough,
you'll find out what makes it tick.

Now the cat's got his tongue.
This is the ritual for the burial of the dead.
Robert Lowell is dead. Tongue-tied.
The homily bubbles over us: the priest conjures
a bell jar. The image is embarrassing.

—Once he fell asleep reading one of my poems
in his office, just before class on Gerald
Warner Brace's couch: "Do you mind if I read
it lying down?" he asks, finishing a sandwich,
propping himself on one elbow. His eyes
close almost instantly. I leave him

for class. Lowell bristles in on time,

alert, heady, rumpled. We spend an hour
on a twelve line poem by Allen Tate lost
down a well.

In the church something is wrong down front:
an usher approaches Elizabeth Hardwick
for Holy Communion; she is standing,
pointing to Caroline Blackwood further down
the front row pew, who declines. Elizabeth
sits down. Neither partakes. Caroline
leads Robert Sheridan Lowell and three
girls up the right aisle, out
of the church. Her high heels click
on the concrete floor like hardtack.
Now we're standing in the aisle, walking
past the vestment-draped coffin, I
touch it barely, I feel the sip
of muscatel going down. I turn and face
the class, pass through the old eyes—

Class is over.
I sit in my seat staring at the Order
for the Burial of the Dead. I translate
the simple German texts: Jesus is here,
Peace and Joy are here. Class is over—
our old rainbow man is gone.
                    Caroline Blackwood
returns, walks with her children to the front
row, sits down. It's over. The mahogany
floats up the aisle without a quiver.
Under the lid, Lowell is rapt, bemused
in his own underworld, no image but his own.
Death at last occurs to him.

Class dismissed. Bach's St. John's Passion
reverberates from every stone. The class

is standing, filing up the aisles,
mute. The passion rocks over the moving
bodies like the sea. Everything is moving.
I can see no faces. A man remains standing
ten pews away, his face in his hand,
weeping. Now he turns,
walks up the aisle, passes
through the doors to the light
outside.

      The women in black
pack into the Cadillac, pass out box
lunches for the trip to Dunbarton, New
Hampshire.

Later a woman critic says Lowell told her
when she scolded such ironic ritual
for backsliders,
          "That's the way we do it."

V

"And so the boy cut down her trunk and made a boat and sailed away."

Shel Silverstein

IN JUNE, THE LEAN CATS IN TENDE

watch for chances from ancient doorways
of the *Rue de France*, and streak
the cobble dark. They are not meek
before the shopper's gait. It is an old play.

Overhead, what's left of the *Chateau Lascaris*
stencils the sky with a slender cornice
ruin, fragile until you see
it up close. A cemetery

of tombs layers to its base
heading up: crushed stone paths
and oval frames with englassed photographs
immaculate in the morning sun, faces

looking in our faces. Below,
the *Roya* cuts the gorge clean,
then under the viaduct and flowing
to the Mediterranean

by the *Hopital Locale*, angling
south. To the north, snow on the Maritime
Alps shows us where we came.
We walk down the back way through tangling

alleys and open kitchen windows, smell fried
meat. The cats are waiting. If we stop
they stab at our sides. Driving, we see the top
of the *Chateau* again—it's ruined side.

PERUGIA, LATE JULY

a. Sunday Morning

Cornflowers tint the weed field blue
and white butterflies tangle-dart in twos
over Queen Anne's lace: the virtue

of a light breeze: neutral space
and buttercups in place
and the buttercups' morning pace.

The grove above the orchard on the nearby hill
is a wasp of pines, as still
as onyx. Here, the cicada double-drills

the drying air, swallows
dart and frolic through the columned tile
and stucco patio. Now church bells

toll from the distant walls
on the other hill.
The field is still.

Soon the tint of blue will
disappear under the rising sun, and the yellow
too. Only white may tell.

b. The Blue Olive Trees at Noon

On this hillside above Ponte san Giovanni
white geese wait in the July
shade. An old man on a balcony

goes into a dark room under the saber
trees: the landscape of black silver, cicada
mint, root bone. In the valley below, the Tiber

curls toward Rome where words add up
to something else. Here the red flags droop
in the sunflower patch and the old man drops

a coil of hose to the ground
and waits. Only the sound
of the cicada thrums these hills crowned

with cypress dark and the sun
bears down on black. Inside the blue tone,
black olives moisten the sun.

c. Sunday Afternoon

The white cocks crow at four
when the sun eases, and geese rouse
gabbling. Beyond our stucco wall, Assisi
clears to an umber

ridge. The wall is so ablaze
and pocked with white, we
squint. Now light bounces to an unglazed
pot of carnations from its clay

water basin: a wisp of white
fire (the secret of green
is black). Orchards of geranium
toll these hillsides bright

with church bells and late swallows
numbered in the softening light.

THE UNICORN IN CAPTIVITY IS

content. His blue field shades
our spun gold ring, you sit
over my pillow biting
your lower lip, weaving our blue
field: I can smell lilies
of the valley, your small bells
of fingers, white horns
braiding to my mouth

we take turns
inside the golden pen, our postcard
by the dresser cockle
bells, your blue gold belt
around my neck. The unicorn is

done for, dressed up
in our clothes, his pricked white
ears and sailing tail through
and through. We are undressed weaving
tapestry bibs. I give you
white, your cockle

lips bell red in a field
of play, flowers blue
yellow all around. The unicorn
in captivity has had it, the game
is up, the place a blue piggley
pen, pomegranates full
to fall, your mouth shaping
the gold circlet
of our den, oh and oh

again, you whisper me death
is kind, my gold eyes open
blind in the valley
of the shadow blue, the killer
flowers under the killer
sun, oh and oh
I am undone.

EXPLORING CAP D'ANTIBES: A GUEST HOUSE, A STUDIO, AN OLD ARBORETUM

and the main gate on the lower road
are all that's left. The man
hauling wood in the shade
does not recognize the names.

We peer in windows when his tractor pulls
away. "The *Garoupe* beach down there
is right," you say. "Mornings he went down to clear
it. Now high surf pounds the trestle

wharf in front of the hotel, and two
lovers hold tight the cable rail,
laughing. They are brown and thin under the blue
morning sky. A warship anchors off *Veille*

Antibes. "There has been a storm at sea."
Three days ago the *Hotel du Roc*
sent us across the road from *Villa Aujourd'hui*
on the curve toward Juan les Pins. The gate was unlocked,

its salmon stucco darkening
in the rain. The new owner knew the owners back
into the twenties. Maurice
Chevalier owned it twenty years. *"Oui. Ici."*

Now above the *Garoupe* beach, the gate
is dark and green. It needs paint.
Gerald Murphy's sign is gone: the faint
evidence of scraped plaster seals its fate.

Half of his paintings are gone
too. Villa America is only a name.
In the *Hotel du Roc*, white leather divans
shine in the immaculate light of dawn.

SHORT STORY

A man lies in a hammock by a hidden
lake at dusk. A light shower
has passed and a school of white
perch spawns a few feet offshore. Their
black fins ripple the surface
of the water. The man shifts to face
the fish, boiling against
the bank, softly agitating his view. He
has come to read: to do

what he will alone, but his book
is closed on his lap and he focuses
this other view. In the end he wants no hocus
pocus of words or hope,
but an exact setting and a tone
of images without dream. A lone heron
wafts from the cove nearby: his eye
stays with the perch snuggling,
percolating under an overhanging birch

where he tied a rowboat as a boy. Then
he knew white perch another way
on a line, the play of hand
to mouth, the struggle of catgut
lip and hook: the trolling strike,
the reel of make believe, pickerel
or bass or that other bass the white
perch, silver and black shining, gills
huffing in crammed buckets, pine spills

sticking to their mucus scaleskins on the ground,
spilled heads. The man
follows the black backs, how they juggle
for unseen positions, toy with water,
liven the shore in a heave of darkening

shine. He has come to take
the place: now the mist
rises, darkness begins. The man walks
the black and silver shore. The contours

fade. *Whippor-whill, whippor-whill.*
He knows there's nothing more.

THE VEIL

is the veil of spring. The green glint
of broken glass on the patio, buttercups
swaying in a light rain, your white

panties hugging. Popponesset
Beach, our old dune, spread-eagling
the eighteen inch crab

in the photograph. Silvertone
and you: *how can I love
you if we do not lie down*, lie

down, lie-down talk early
in the fifties. The veil is
the veil of talk, what I heard

in a dream: *I know a softer game
than this*, and thought it
was you but it was only me talking

to myself. So in that other dream
last year, standing in the long
line, stepping inside the ancient

chamber, dropping a thousand
years over the tournament field,
breast-powering

over the martial parade, heading
straight up in the bachelor-
button blue and the banner unfurled

with the message *come
back*. It was no birch
dipping. The veil

77

is the veil of memory. I
love the veils. Yet I would peel
them in a land of no talk, no blue

in the chalk trees, no belly
tonguing on the long white beach
for a true inside voice, even my own.

LEANING OVER THE WHARF IN BIMINI

we watch the queen triggerfish nibble the piling
stalks and the channel tide
sweep our brown rice and peas over the smiling
smallmouth grunts cruising bottom-eyed

unattended, random, gone in the flow. We
have come to sit in the sun at noon
on the wharf in the turquoise channel and maybe
see the great rays burst up in their roundspoon

forms, straight up only to fall
in a white fluttering smash almost too quick
to catch with the eye unless glued beforehand to the small
zone where that concentration picked

up and left off, or leap on a curve
with a blast-out flapping thrust and flap
again its rug-like self and heavy downswerve
into the ripple surface lap

of the channel tide. Yesterday I saw
that very leap, now a seeming dream. We
mark the soft emerald tint, then sapphire, and draw
the bottom where the sand gives way to grass. When he

appears we are not ready and we start.
"Look," you point, and the black shroud moves
across the bottom grandly, blackly, wingparts
undulating softly at the tips toward us smooth

black and turning, sweeps into the dark
reflecting waters of the sun. Now an angelfish
appears and one harlequin bass, and we turn to mark
a pelican overhead who casts a shadow. We each make a wish.

FEVERFEW, BOOK-MOTH, AND FATE

Crawling the middle lane of the YMCA pool
at noon, I lap the blind girl

backstroking serenely along the side wall
tile. Occasionally we touch as her arms mill

the wide arc of her water thrash, hand
to foot or foot to hand. Her other hand

fingertips the tile wall although I cannot see
that braille. I am eyeing

the yellow space between the bottom lines,
glimpsing the yellow air in my breathing turns,

resolving my own riddle of the healing
pool, closing the gaps of my daily quarter mile.

I do not know how far she has to go.
We touch again. She does not know

that the stitch in my side is healing,
that I believe the deer finds the hunter kneeling

in the yellow woods to rest, that I read
this morning that plantain and feverfew and the red

nettle that grows in the house, all
boiled in butter will also ease the travail

of the sudden stitch, even that the glories of Christ
are great but that *wyrd* is mightiest.

Fate: so think I, crawling in the healing pool
past the blind girl serene. I the fool

Anglo-Saxon who reads the *Exeter Book* before my swim
for a charm, the *Cotton Manuscript* for a maxim.

Here in these yellow waters end to end
where the spring sun is another form of let's pretend,

I remember the book-moth charm and ponder
the poet's seeming of a marvelous thing, the wonder

that a worm has swallowed, in darkness stolen
the song of a man, and a woman.